To Kit
from
Mary
Summer '97

# Happiness

First published in Great Britain in 1996 by
BROCKHAMPTON PRESS
20 Bloomsbury Street, London WC1B 3QA
a member of the Hodder Headline Group

This series of little gift books was made by Frances Banfield, Andrea P.A. Belloli, Polly Boyd,
Kate Brown, Stefano Carantino, Laurel Clark, Penny Clarke, Clive Collins, Jack Cooper, Melanie Cumming,
Nick Diggory, John Dunne, Deborah Gill, David Goodman, Paul Gregory, Douglas Hall, Lucinda Hawksley,
Maureen Hill, Dennis Hovell, Dicky Howett, Nick Hutchison, Douglas Ingram, Helen Johnson, C.M. Lee,
Simon London, Irene Lyford, John Maxwell, Patrick McCreeth, Morse Modaberi, Tara Neill, Sonya Newland,
Anne Newman, Grant Oliver, Ian Powling, Terry Price, Michelle Rogers, Mike Seabrook,
Nigel Soper, Karen Sullivan and Nick Wells.

# CELEBRATION

# *Happiness*

Selected by Karen Sullivan

## BROCKHAMPTON PRESS

A. Barrère

MARGUERITE DEVAL    FUGÈRE    FRAGSON    OTÉRO

# LA REVUE DES FOLI

Our brightest blazes of gladness
are commonly kindled by
unexpected sparks.

Samuel Johnson

When we are happy we are always
good, but when we are good we
are not always happy.

Oscar Wilde

1

Happiness makes up in height what it lacks in length.

Robert Frost

My heart leaps up when I behold
A rainbow in the sky:
So was it when my life began;
So is it now I am a man:
So be it when I shall grow old,
Or let me die!
The child is father of the man;
And I could wish my days to be
Bound each to each by natural piety.

William Wordsworth

It is impossible for a man to be made happy by putting him in a happy place, unless he be first in a happy state.

Benjamin Whichcote, *Moral and Religious Aphorisms*

'Oh, Matthew, isn't it a wonderful morning? The world looks like something God had just imagined for His own pleasure!'

L. M. Montgomery, *Anne of Green Gables*

Some cause happiness wherever they go; others whenever they go.

Anonymous

Sir, that all who are happy,
are equally happy, is not
true. A peasant and a
philosopher may be equally
satisfied, but not equally
happy. Happiness consists
in the multiplicity of
agreeable consciousness.

Samuel Johnson

Happiness seems made to
be shared.

Jean Racine

# Fine Fun

A Volume of Coloured Pictures and Stories

ERNEST NISTER. LONDON.

E. P. DUTTON & CO. NEW

The supreme happiness of life is the conviction of being loved for yourself, or, more correctly, being loved in spite of yourself.

Victor Hugo

He who regards the world as he does the fortunes of his own body can govern the world. He who loves the world as he does his own body can be entrusted with the world.

Lao Tsu, *Tao Te Ching*

It seldom happens that any felicity comes so pure as not to be
tempered and allayed by some mixture of sorrow.

Miguel de Cervantes


Happy the man, and happy he alone,
He who can call today his own;
He who, secure within, can say,
Tomorrow, do thy worst, for I have lived today.

John Dryden

I wandered lonely as a cloud
That floats on high o'er vales and hills,
When all at once I saw a crowd,
A host, of golden daffodils;
Beside the lake, beneath the trees,
Fluttering and dancing in the breeze.

Continuous as the stars that shine
And twinkle on the milky way.
They stretched in never-ending line
Along the margin of a bay:
Ten thousand saw I at a glance,
Tossing their heads in sprightly dance.

The waves beside them danced; but they
Out-did the sparkling waves in glee:
A poet could not but be gay,
In such a jocund company:
I gazed – and gazed – but little thought
What wealth the show to me had brought:

For oft, when on my couch I lie
In vacant or in pensive mood,
They flash upon that inward eye
Which is the bliss of solitude;
And then my heart with pleasure fills,
And dances with the daffodils.

William Wordsworth, *'Daffodils'*

Happiness is having a large, loving, caring, close-knit family in another city.

George Burns

There is something ridiculous and even quite indecent in an individual claiming to be happy. Still more a people or a nation making such a claim. The pursuit of happiness… is without any question the most fatuous which could possibly be undertaken. This lamentable phrase 'the pursuit of happiness' is responsible for a good part of the ills and miseries of the modern world.

Malcolm Muggeridge

Same old slippers,
Same old rice,
Same old glimpse of
Paradise.

William James Lampton

True happiness is of a retired
nature, and an enemy to
pomp and noise.

Joseph Addison

17

Perfect happiness, even in memory, is not common.

Jane Austen, *Emma*

To enjoy true happiness we must travel into a very far country,
and even out of ourselves.

Sir Thomas Browne, *Christian Morals*

There comes
For ever something between us and what
We deem our happiness.

Lord Byron, *Sardanapalus*

Happiness in this world, when it comes, comes incidentally. Make it the object of pursuit, and it leads us on a wild-goose chase, and is never attained. Follow some other object, and very possibly we may find that we have caught happiness without dreaming of it.

Nathaniel Hawthorne, *American Notebooks*

Guard within yourself that treasure, kindness. Know how to give without hesitation, how to lose without regret, how to acquire without meanness; how to replace in your heart, by the happiness of those you love, the happiness that may be wanting to yourself.

George Sand

# The Garden Coach.

*HI!* hi! clear the way,
　　This is the garden coach;
　It starts at morn,
　They blow the horn,
To herald its approach!

Hi! hi! shout hurrah!
Baby is off to Town,
　　With coat and cape
　　Of proper shape,
A coachman of renown!

Hi! hi! jump up, guard!
Blow on your horn and tell
　　The neighbours all,
　　Both great and small,
You know your duties well!

Hi! hi! crack the whip.
"Isn't it time
　　　to start?"
"I'm ready now,"
Says Spot,
　　　"bow-wow—
　The coach should
　　now depart!"

Hi! hi! off it goes!
Cracking his whip,
　　　says he,
"You'll have
　　to run,
　We dine
　　at one—
And hungry
　we shall be!"

C. B.

Margaret seemed to find it a little hard to tell hers, and moved a brake before her face, as if to disperse imaginary gnats, while she said, slowly, 'I should like a lovely house, full of all sorts of luxurious things; nice food, pretty clothes, handsome furniture, pleasant people, and heaps of money. I am to be mistress of it, and manage it as I like, with plenty of servants, so I never need work a bit. How I should enjoy it! for I wouldn't be idle, but do good, and make everyone love me dearly.'

Louisa May Alcott, *Little Women*

When a baby first looks at you; when it gets excited at seeing a ray of light and like a dog pawing a gleam, tries to capture it in his hand; or when it laughs that deep, unselfconscious gurgle; or when it cries and you pick it up and it clings sobbing to you, saved from some terrible shadow moving across the room, or a loud clang in the street, or perhaps, already, a bad dream: then you are – happy is not the precise word – filled... she felt she lived at the blind true core of life.

Marilyn French, *The Women's Room*

23

All people smile in the same language.

American proverb

Human felicity is produced not so much by great pieces of good fortune that seldom happen, as by little advantages that occur every day.

Benjamin Franklin

A poor life this if, full of care,
We have no time to stand and stare.

W. H. Davies, *Leisure*

Happiness is good health and a bad memory.

Ingrid Bergman

Here with a Loaf of Bread beneath the Bough,
A Flask of Wine, a Book of Verse – and Thou
Beside me singing in the Wilderness –
And Wilderness is Paradise enow.

Edward FitzGerald, *The Rubaiyat of Omar Khayyam*

THE ILLUSTRATED LONDON NEWS WEDDING NUMBER, APRIL 28, 1923.—729

# Happiness

Hear the mellow wedding bells,
Golden bells!
What a world of happiness their harmony foretells!
E. A. Poe.

WEDDING BELLS ring out the message of Happiness—the most precious of all human blessings.

Happiness should be the treasured possession of everyone. Many are the obstacles and hindrances, and of these possibly the most important is lack of health. For Happiness and Health go hand in hand.

It is the privilege of "Ovaltine" to make an important contribution to the sum of human happiness. For this delicious beverage gives and maintains Health.

"Ovaltine" is a concentrated extraction of all the goodness, all the nutriment, all the health-giving properties contained in ripe barley malt, rich creamy milk, and fresh eggs—Nature's Tonic Foods. It contains all the vitamines essential for the nourishment, protection and health of the body.

Drink "Ovaltine" as your daily beverage—for Health! It gives strength and vitality, restores in fatigue, and fortifies the system against colds and more serious ailments. It is splendid for children, too, building up healthy bodies and promoting sturdy muscular development. Drink it as a "night-cap" to ensure sound, natural sleep.

Sold by all Chemists and Stores at 1/6, 2/6 and 4/6.
It is economical to purchase the larger sized tins.

A. WANDER, LTD., 45, Cowcross St., London, E.C.1.
Works: King's Langley.

P 230

## Health and Happiness go hand in hand with "Ovaltine"

There are two things to aim at in life: first, to get what you want; and, after that, to enjoy it. Only the wisest of mankind achieve the second.

Logan Pearsall Smith

The history of the world is not the theatre of happiness. Periods of happiness are blank pages in it, for they are periods of harmony – periods when the antithesis is in abeyance.

Georg Hegel

Happiness is the only sanction of life; where happiness fails, existence remains a mad and lamentable experiment.

George Santayana

There is no duty we so much underrate as the duty of being happy.

Robert Louis Stevenson, *Virginibus Puerisque*

Those who weep for the happy periods which they encounter in history acknowledge what they want; not the alleviation but the silencing of misery.

Albert Camus

'What is the secret of your life?' asked Mrs Browning of Charles Kingsley. 'Tell me, that I may make mine beautiful too.' He replied, 'I had a friend.'

William C. Gannet

Now may the warming love of friends
Surround you as you go
Down the path of light and laughter
Where the happy memories grow

Helen Lowrie Marshall


Who is the happiest of men?
He who values the merits of others
And in their pleasure takes joy,
Even as though it were his own.

Goethe

That is the land of lost content,
I see it shining plain,
The happy highways where I went
And cannot come again.

A. E. Housman

God speaks to us in our joy but shouts to us in our pain.

Anonymous

I have known laughter – therefore I may sorrow with you
more tenderly…

William Lloyd Garrison

To laugh often and much; to win the respect of intelligent people and the affection of children; to earn the appreciation of honest critics, and endure the betrayal of false friends; to appreciate beauty; to find the best in others; to leave the world a bit better whether by a healthy child, a garden patch, or a redeemed social condition; to know even one life has breathed easier because you have lived. This is to have success.

Ralph Waldo Emerson

If you would be happy for a week kill a pig; if you would be happy for a month take a wife; but if you would be happy all your life, plant a garden.

Proverb

Life itself is the real and most miraculous miracle of all. If anyone had never before seen a human hand and were suddenly presented for the first time with this strange and wonderful thing, what a miracle, what a magnificently shocking and inexplicable and mysterious thing it would be. In my plays I want to look at life – at the commonplace of existence – as if we had just turned a corner and run into it for the first time.

Christopher Fry, *Time* magazine

I have wanted only one thing to keep me happy, but wanting that have wanted everything.

William Hazlitt, *Winterslow*

WHIRLIGIG PICTURES

London.
Ernest Nister

Printed in Bavaria.
261

New York.
E. P. Dutton & Co

We love life, not because we are used to living, but because we are used to loving.

Friedrich Nietzsche, *Thus Spake Zarathustra*

Life is to be fortified by many friendships. To love and to be loved is the greatest happiness in existence.

Sydney Smith

Life at its noblest leaves mere happiness far behind; and indeed cannot endure it... Happiness is not the object of life: life has no object: it is an end in itself; and courage consists in the readiness to sacrifice happiness for an intenser quality of life.

George Bernard Shaw

Today a new sun rises for me; everything lives, everything is animated, everything seems to speak to me of my passion, everything invites me to cherish it...

Anne de Lenclos

He is the happiest man who can trace an unbroken connection between the end of his life and the beginning.

Goethe, *Maxims and Reflections*

Believe each day that has dawned to be your last. Some hour to which you have not been looking forward will prove lovely.

Horace, *Epistles*

Joy seems to me a stop
beyond happiness –
happiness is a sort of
atmosphere you can live
in sometimes when you
are lucky. Joy is a light
that fills you with hope
and faith and love.

Adela Rogers St Johns

Happiness is a mystery,
like religion, and should
never be rationalized.

G. K. Chesterton

It seems to me you can be awfully happy in this life if you stand aside and watch and mind your own business and let other people do as they like about damaging themselves and one another. You go on kidding yourself that you're impartial and tolerant and all that, then all of a sudden you realize you're dead, and you've never been alive at all.

Mary Stewart, *This Rough Magic*

How good it feels – the hand of an old friend.

Henry Wadsworth Longfellow

# A CARRIAGE AND PAIR

A PICTURE BOOK
FOR LITTLE FOLK

London
Ernest Nister

Printed in Bavaria

New York.
E. P. Dutton & Co.

Life is bliss; no person need suffer any more.

Maharishi Mahesh Yogi

It is eternity now. I am in the midst of it. It is about me in the sunshine; I am in it, as the butterfly in the light-laden air. Nothing has to come; it is now. Now is eternity; now is the immortal life.

Richard Jefferies, *The Story of My Heart*

Happiness is no laughing matter.

Richard Whately, *Apophthegms*

 47

The best portion of a good man's life –
His little, nameless, unremembered acts
Of kindness and of love.

William Wordsworth

I am grown peaceful as old age tonight;
I regret a little, I would change still less.

Robert Browning, *Andrea del Sarto*

To be able to enjoy one's past life is to live twice.

Martial

Happiness is not having what you want, but wanting what you have.

Hyman Judha Schachtel, *Real Enjoyment of Living*

Happiness was not made to be boasted, but enjoyed. Therefore tho' others count me miserable, I will not believe them if I know and feel myself to be happy; nor fear them.

Thomas Traherne

We are never happy; we can only remember that we were so once.

Alexander Smith

Happy he who like Ulysses has made a great journey.

Joachim du Bellay

He who has once been happy is for aye'
Out of destruction's reach.

Wilfred Scawen Blunt, *Esther*

Point me out the happy man and I will point you out either egotism,
selfishness, evil – or else an absolute ignorance.

Graham Greene

The actual experience of being a mother is one of the most fulfilling I've ever had. Pregnancy was the most continuous happiness I've known. Each time I've experienced birth there's been an overbearing feeling of loss, in the hospital right after the baby's birth, when the baby would be taken into the nursery.

And then the greatest flooding of joy when the baby would be brought back to me.

Gloria Vanderbilt, *Woman to Woman*

They seemed to come suddenly upon happiness as if they had surprised a butterfly in the winter woods...

Edith Wharton

Joy is prayer – Joy is strength – Joy is love – Joy is a net of love by which you can catch souls. God loves a cheerful giver. She gives most who gives with joy. The best way to show our gratitude to God and the people is to accept everything with joy. A joyful heart is the inevitable result of a heart burning with love. Never let anything so fill you with sorrow as to make you forget the joy of the Christ risen.

Mother Teresa

The excursion is the same when you go looking for your sorrow as when you go looking for your joy.

Eudora Welty

Happiness is white and pink.

Théopile Gautier, *Caprices et zigzags*

If happiness is activity in accordance with excellence,
it is reasonable that it should be in accordance with
the highest excellence.

Aristotle

It is neither wealth nor splendour, but tranquillity
and occupation, which give happiness.

Thomas Jefferson, Letter, 1788

The world is so full of a number of things,
I'm sure we should all be as happy as kings.

Robert Louis Stevenson, *A Child's Garden of Verses*

A merry heart makes a cheerful countenance.

*Proverbs*, XV:13

There are people who can do all fine and heroic things but one:
keep from telling their happinesses to the unhappy.

Mark Twain

And those that were good shall be happy: they shall sit in a golden chair;
They shall splash at a ten-league canvas with brushes of comet's hair.

Rudyard Kipling, *When Earth's Last Picture is Painted*

Happiness consumes itself like a flame. It cannot burn for ever, it must
go out, and the presentiment of its end destroys it at its very peak.

J. August Strindberg

Unbroken happiness is a bore: it should have its ups and downs.

Molière, *Les Fourberies de Scapin*

Happiness is an imaginary condition, formerly often
attributed by the living to the dead, now usually attributed
by adults to children, and by children to adults.

Thomas Szasz


Happiness is a wine of the rarest vintage, and seems
insipid to a vulgar taste.

Logan Pearsall Smith


I must go down to the sea again, to the lonely sea and the sky,
And all I ask is a tall ship and a star to steer her by,
And the wheel's kick and the wind's song and the white sail's shaking,
And a grey mist on the sea's face and a grey dawn breaking.

John Masefield, *'Sea Fever'*

We all want to be happy, and we're all going to die…
You might say those are the only two unchallengeably
true facts that apply to every human being on this planet.

William Boyd


Your joy is your own; your bitterness is your own.
No one can share them with you.

Proverb


You never enjoy the world aright, till the sea itself floweth
in your veins, till you are clothed with the heavens and
crowned with the stars.

Thomas Traherne

Let us be grateful to people who make us happy; they are
the charming gardeners who make our souls blossom.

Marcel Proust

Let no man be called happy before his death. Till then,
he is not happy, only lucky.

Solon

Laughter may hide sadness. When happiness is gone,
sorrow is always there.

Proverb

# The Dandy Chair.

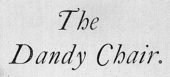

THE birds
   were telling
The time of day,
"What do you
         think?"
   I heard
      one say,
"I saw
   this morning
      over there—
A little maid
   in a Dandy
         Chair!"

"I wish,"
   the next said,
"I'd been there,
It's nice to ride
         in a
      Dandy Chair!"
"I saw it also,"
      cried a third,
"She looked
   as happy as a bird!"

He there does now enjoy eternal rest
And happie ease, which thou doest want and crave,
And further from it daily wanderest.

Edmund Spenser, *'The Fairie Queene'*

My mind to me a kingdom is,
Such present joys therein I find,
That it excels all other bliss
That earth affords or grows by kind.

Edward Dyer, *My Mind to Me a Kingdom Is*

Happy are those
Who reject the advice of evil men,
Who do not follow the example of sinners
Or join those who have no use for God.

*Psalms*

Oh happy who thus liveth,
Not caring much for gold,
With clothing which sufficeth
To keep from him the cold.
Though poor and plain his diet
Yet merry it is and quiet.

Anonymous, *'The Herdsman'*

Hope is itself a species of happiness, and, perhaps, the chief happiness which this world affords: but, like all other pleasures immoderately enjoyed, the excesses of hope must be expiated by pain; and expectations improperly indulged must end in disappointment.

Samuel Johnson

Happiness ain't a thing in itself – it's only a contrast with something that ain't pleasant… And so, as soon as the novelty is over and the force of the contrast dulled, it ain't happiness any longer, and you have to get something fresh.

Mark Twain

True happiness consists not in the multitude of friends, but in the worth and choice.

Ben Johnson

Happiness is always a by-product. It is probably a matter of temperament, and for anything I know it may be glandular. But it is not something that can be demanded from life, and if you are not happy you had better stop worrying about it and see what treasures you can pluck from your own brand of unhappiness.

Robertson Davies

That action is best which procures the greatest happiness for the greatest numbers.

Francis Hutcheson, *Concerning Moral Good and Evil*

We are made happy when reason can discover no occasion for it. The memory of some past moments is more persuasive than the experience of present ones. There have been visions of such breadth and brightness that these motes were invisible in their light.

Henry David Thoreau

Virtue is simply happiness, and happiness is a by-product of function. You are happy when you are functioning.

William Burroughs

I earn that I eat,
get that I wear,
owe no man hate,
envy no man's
happiness, glad
of other men's
good, content with
my harm.

William Shakespeare,
*As You Like It*

To be good is to
be happy.

Nicholas Rowe,
*The Fair Penitent*

MERRY PLAYHOURS

E Stewart

Ernest Nister, London.          Printed in Bavaria          E.P. Dutton & Co.
                                      151

For all the happiness mankind can gain
Is not in pleasure, but in rest from pain.

John Dryden, *The Indian Emperor*


The sum of earthly bliss.
In solitude
What happiness? Who can enjoy alone,
Or all enjoying, what contentment find?

John Milton, *'Paradise Lost'*


O Happiness! our being's end and aim,
Good, pleasure, ease, content! whate'er thy name:
That something still which prompts th'eternal sigh,
For which we bear to live, or dare to die.

Alexander Pope, *An Essay on Man*

All who would win joy must share it;
happiness was born a twin.

Lord Byron

Where ignorance is bliss, 'tis folly to be wise.

Proverb

But if this be not happiness – who knows?
Some day I shall think this a happy day,
And this mood by the name of melancholy
Shall no more blackened and obscurèd be.

Edward Thomas, *October*

In the
Swing.

Breathless, we flung us on the windy hill,
Laughed in the sun, and kissed the lovely grass.

Rupert Brooke, *'The Hill'*

Earthlier happy is the rose distill'd
Than that which withering on the virgin thorn,
Grows, lives, and dies in single blessedness.

William Shakespeare, *A Midsummer-Night's Dream*

That thou art happy, owe to God.

John Milton, *'Paradise Lost'*

## Notes on Illustrations

**Page 1** *La Revue des Folies-Bergere* by Adrien Barrere (Private Collection). Courtesy of The Bridgeman Art Library; **Page 2** *Something Nice for Dobbin.* Courtesy of The Laurel Clark Collection; **Page 5** *The Cradle* by Berthe Morisot (Musee d'Orsay, Paris). Courtesy of The Bridgeman Art Library; **Page 7** *Sunset* by George Pierre Seurat (City of Bristol Museum and Art Gallery). Courtesy of The Bridgeman Art Library; **Page 8** *Fine Fun.* Courtesy of The Laurel Clark Collection; **Page 11** *The Rehearsal* by Edgar Degas (Burrell Collection, Glasgow). Courtesy of The Bridgeman Art Library; **Page 14** *Design for Playbill for The Bluebird* by Frederick Cayley Robinson (Haymarket Theatre, London). Courtesy of The Bridgeman Art Library; **Page 16** *Sleep Baby Sleep* by Willebeek Mair (Private Collection). Courtesy of The Bridgeman Art Library; **Page 19** *The Happy Mag.* Courtesy of The Laurel Clark Collection; **Page 21** *The Garden Coach.* Courtesy of The Laurel Clark Collection; **Page 24** *The Apple Gatherers* by Frederick Morgan (Roy Miles Gallery, 29 Bruton Street, London). Courtesy of The Bridgeman Art Library; **Page 27** *Sweethearts, from the Pears Annual* by Frederick Morgan (A & F Pears Ltd., London). Courtesy of The Bridgeman Art Library; **Page 28** *Health and Happiness Go Hand in Hand with Ovaltine.* Courtesy of The Laurel Clark Collection; **Page 31** *Awake* by Sophie Anderson (Christopher Wood Gallery, London). Courtesy of The Bridgeman Art Library; **Page 33** *Singin' in the Rain.* Courtesy of The Laurel Clark Collection; **Page 34** *The Terrace at Ste. Adresse Near Le Havre* by Claude Monet (Metropolitan Museum of Art, New York). Courtesy of The Bridgeman Art Library; **Page 38** *Whirligig Pictures.* Courtesy of The Laurel Clark Collection; **Page 41** *The Promised Paradise Beyond the Mountains, Flute Player and Children* by Kate Greenaway (Private Collection). Courtesy of The Bridgeman Art Library; **Pages 42-3** *Poster for Barnum and Bailey's Circus* (Private Collection). Courtesy of The Bridgeman Art Library; **Page 45** *A Carriage and Pair.* Courtesy of The Laurel Clark Collection; **Page 46** *Dancers in Blue* by Edgar Degas (Musée d'Orsay, Paris). Courtesy of The Bridgeman Art Library; **Page 48** *Playtime of Life, Away from all Strife* (Private Collection). Courtesy of The Bridgeman Art Library; **Page 51** *A Flushed and Boisterous Group* by Arthur Rackham (Private Collection). Courtesy of The Bridgeman Art Library; **Page 52** *Building the Snowman.* Courtesy of The Laurel Clark Collection; **Page 56** *Woman with Parasol Turned Left* by Claude Monet (Musée d'Orsay, Paris). Courtesy of The Bridgeman Art Library; **Page 59** *Children Dancing Round the Christmas Tree.* Courtesy of The Laurel Clark Collection; **Page 60** *The Happy Mag – Extra Holiday Number.* Courtesy of The Laurel Clark Collection; **Page 62** *Children with Lambs Among the Daisies* by Mary Ellen Edwards (Private Collection). Courtesy of The Bridgeman Art Library; **Page 64** *A Street in Clovelly* by Edward Wilkins Waite (Private Collection). Courtesy of The Bridgeman Art Library; **Page 67** *The Dandy Chair.* Courtesy of The Laurel Clark

Collection; **Page 71** *Three Dancers in Peasant Costume* by Edgar Degas (Private Collection). Courtesy of The Bridgeman Art Library; **Page 73** *Happy Thoughts.* Courtesy of The Laurel Clark Collection; **Page 74** *On the Beach.* Courtesy of The Laurel Clark Collection; **Pages 76-7** *Ringling Bros Shows – The World's Greatest Circus* (Private Collection). Courtesy of The Bridgeman Art Library; **Page 78** *Merry Playhours.* Courtesy of The Laurel Clark Collection; **Page 81** *The Dancing Class* by Edgar Degas (Musee d'Orsay, Paris). Courtesy of The Bridgeman Art Library; **Page 82** *In the Swing.* Courtesy of The Laurel Clark Collection.

Acknowledgements: The Publishers wish to thank everyone who gave permission to reproduce the quotes in this book. Every effort has been made to contact the copyright holders, but in the event that an oversight has occurred, the publishers would be delighted to rectify any omissions in future editions of this book. Robert Frost from *The Poetry of Robert Frost,* reprinted by permission of Jonathan Cape, the Estate of Robert Frost and Peter A. Gilbert, North Hampshire, USA © Robert Frost; G. K. Chesterton reprinted courtesy of Methuen and Dodd Mead, copyright renewed; *Anne of Green Gables,* by L. M. Montgomery, reprinted courtesy of Sterling Publishing Limited; W. H. Davies, from *The Complete Poems of W. H. Davies,* published by Jonathan Cape, reprinted courtesy of the executors of the W. H. Davies estate, copyright renewed; Rudyard Kipling, reprinted courtesy of Macmillan Publishing Company Limited; John Masefield, reprinted courtesy of Reed Books and the Literary Trustees of John Masefield and The Society of Authors as their representative; Gloria Vanderbilt, from *Woman to Woman,* reprinted courtesy of Garden City and Doubleday; Ogden Nash, from *Verses from 1929 on* reprinted by permission of Curtis Brown, Ltd. Copyright © 1942 by Ogden Nash, renewed; *Good News Study Bible,* published by Thomas Nelson, 1986, extracts reprinted with their kind permission; *Penguin Book of Japanese Verse,* translated by Geoffrey Bownas and Anthony Thwaite, published by Penguin 1964, and reprinted with their permission.